Miami Lakes

TOWN OF
MIAMI
LAKES

From A to Z

By Gael Daly

Find the alphabet letters in the pictures of
Miami Lakes, learn about the town and enjoy a
joke or riddle on every page.

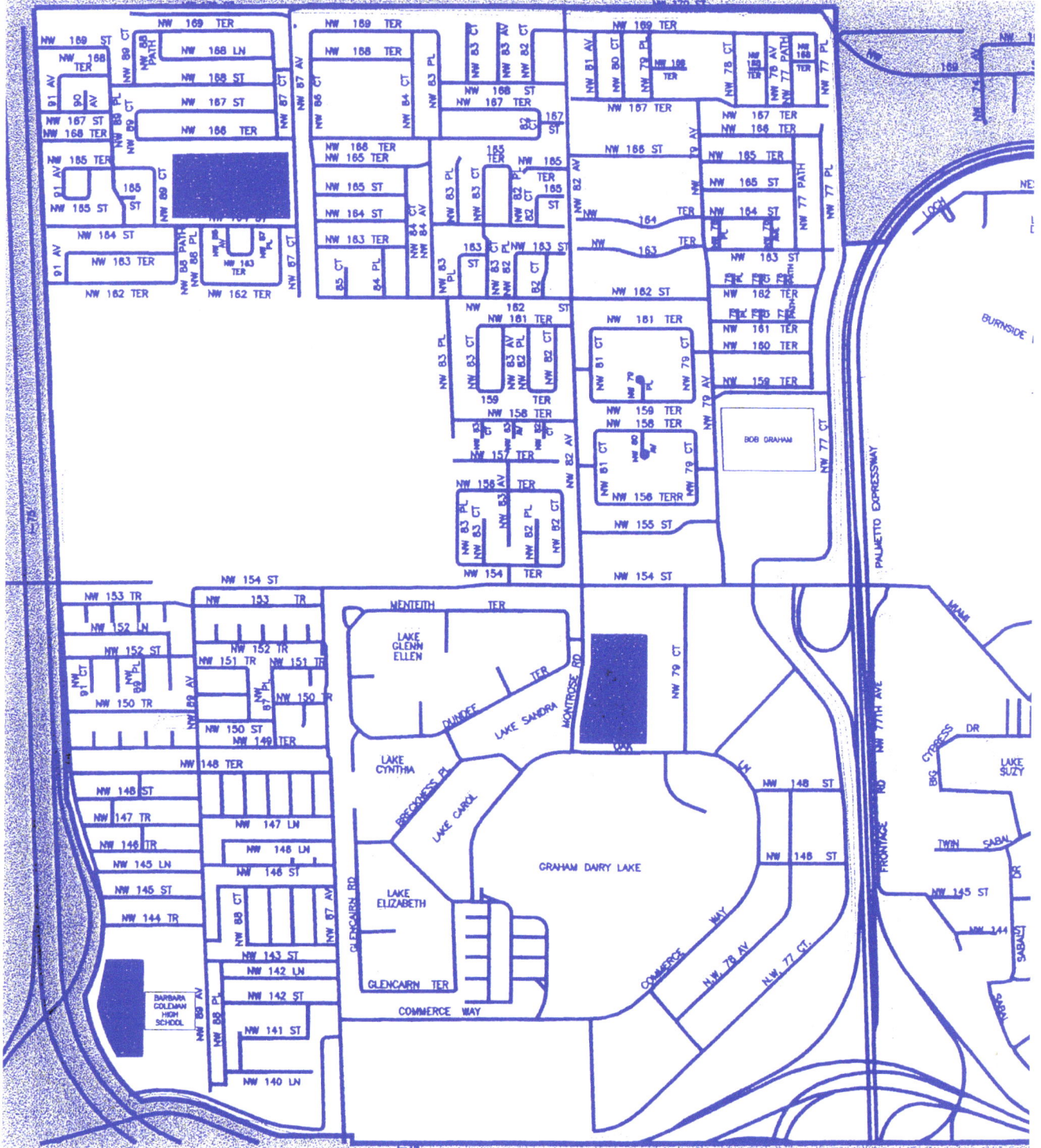

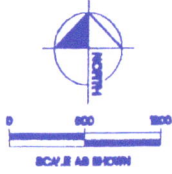

Town Map

NW 169 ST
NW 169 TER
NW 169 TER
NW 170

NW 168 TER
NW 88 PATH
NW 168 LN
NW 188 TER
NW 81 AV
NW 80 CT
NW 79 PL
NW 78 CT
NW 79 AV
NW 77 PATH
NW 77 PL

NW 91 AV
NW 90 AV
NW 168 ST
NW 87 AV
NW 86 CT
NW 167 TER
NW 168 TER
NW 187 ST
NW 167 TER
NW 167 ST
NW 186 TER
NW 157 TER
NW 157 TER
NW 166 TER

NW 185 TER
NW 168 TER
NW 165 TER
NW 166 ST
NW 165 ST
NW 165 ST

NW 91 AV
NW 185 ST
NW 185 ST
NW 165 TER
NW 83 CT
NW 82 PL
NW 82 AV
NW 164 TER
NW 164 ST
NW 77 PATH
NW 77 PL

NW 184 ST
NW 89 CT
NW 184 ST
NW 184 TER
NW 164 TER
NW 163

NW 91 AV
NW 163 TER
NW 88 PATH
NW 88 PL
NW 143 TER
NW 87 CT
NW 83 CT
NW 83 ST
NW 183 ST
NW 163
NW 183 ST

NW 162 TER
NW 162 TER
NW 85 CT
NW 84 PL
NW 83 PL
NW 83 ST
NW 182 ST
NW 182 ST
NW 161 ST
NW 161 TER
NW 161 TER
NW 160 TER

NW 182 ST
NW 161 TER
NW 83 CT
NW 83 AV
NW 82 CT
NW 82 ST
NW 81 CT
NW 79 CT
NW 79 AV
NW 159 TER

NW 159
NW 159 TER
NW 158 TER
NW 159 TER
NW 158 TER

NW 157 TER
NW 81 CT
NW 80
NW 79
NW 156 TER
BOB GRAHAM
NW 77 CT

NW 156 AV
NW 83 PL
NW 83 CT
NW 82 PL
NW 82 CT
NW 155 ST

NW 154 TER
NW 154 ST
NW 154 ST

NW 153 TR
NW 153 TR
MENTEITH TER

NW 152 LN
LAKE GLENN ELLEN

NW 152 ST
NW 152 TR
NW 151 TR
NW 151 TR
TER

NW 91 CT
NW 150 TR
NW 150 TR
DUNDEE
LAKE SANDRA
MONTROSE RD
NW 79 CT

NW 150 ST
NW 149 TER

NW 148 TER
LAKE CYNTHIA
BRECKNESS PL
NW 148 ST
NW 148 ST

NW 148 ST
LAKE CAROL
NW 147 TR
NW 147 LN
NW 148 ST

NW 146 TR
NW 148 LN
NW 146 ST
GRAHAM DAIRY LAKE
NW 145 ST

NW 145 LN
NW 146 ST
NW 144

NW 145 ST
LAKE ELIZABETH

NW 144 TR
NW 88 CT
NW 87 AV
COMMERCE WAY
NW 78 AV
NW 77 CT

BARBARA GOLDMAN HIGH SCHOOL
NW 143 ST
NW 142 LN
NW 142 ST
GLENCAIRN TER
GLENCAIRN RD

NW 88 PL
NW 86 AV
NW 141 ST
COMMERCE WAY

NW 140 LN

I-75

PALMETTO EXPRESSWAY
BURNSIDE
LOCH
MIAMI
NW 77TH AVE
FRONTAGE RD
CYPRESS DR
BIG
LAKE SUZY
TWIN
SABAL
NW 145 ST
SABAL

NORTH

0   600   1200
SCALE AS SHOWN

PALMETTO EXPRESSWAY

NW 167 ST

NW 185 TER
NW 163 ST
NW 59 AV
NW 58 AV
NW 158 ST
NW 59 AV

DUNOON CT
HAVEN
STONE RD
LOCH NESS
LOCH DOON
GLENEAGLE DR
LOCH LOMOND
TORPHIN PL
E TROON CIR
ABERDEEN WY
KINGSMOOR WY
W PRESTWICK PL
TROON CIR
W TROON
GORNOCH RND
BERWICK WY
TURNBERRY DR
S PRESTWICK PL
CROWN GATE DR
BATH RD
LAKEWAY RD

MILK WAGON LANE
BRIAR PATCH PL
COTTON TAIL ROAD

MIAMI LAKES MIDDLE SCHOOL
OUR LADY OF THE LAKES SCHOOL
MONTESSORI SCHOOL
MIAMI LAKES VOCATIONAL CENTER

MIAMI LAKEWAY N
EAGLE NEST LN
COWPEN RD
THURNBULL DR
RUSHMORE DR
BULL RUN
MAIN ST
NEW BARN RD
BULL RUN RD
EAGLE NEST LN
MOULTRIE PL
PENT PL
MIAMI LAKES DR
EGAN LN

NW 153 ST
NW 151 ST
NW 57TH CT
MIAMI LAKES DRIVE
NW 60TH AVE

FAIRWAY
DRIVE
HOLLY RD
LAURELLN
MIAMI LAKES DR
QUEEN PALM TER
LAKE MARTHA
CASSIA PL
BOTTLE BRUSH TER
PALMETTO PALM DR
PARKINSONIA
ORCHID DR
LAKES
MONKSWOOD
RIDGEWOOD BLVD
DADE
MAPLE TER
CEDAR CT
PINE
WILLOW LN
TABEBUIA
MIAMI LAKEWAY S
MIAMI LAKES ELEMENTARY SCHOOL
LAKE COMO TER
LAKE BLUE DR
WHITE OAK DR

LAKE KATHERINE
LEWIS PL
FITZPATRICK RD
ENGLISH RD
LAKEWAY S
LAKE GENEVA RD
LAKE CANDLEWOOD PL
LAKE ORCHARD CT
LAKE CHAMPLAIN TER
LAKE PATRICIA

NW 146 ST
NW 142 ST
NW 139 ST

LAKE SARAH
LEANING PINE DR
PINE CT
SILVER
OAK DR
LAKE HILDA
CROOKED PALM LN
CROOKED PALM TER
LAKE
LAKE ADELA
CYPRESS CT
ALAMANDA
SEA GRAPE TER
BAMBOO ST

LAKE PATRICIA
LAKE DUCLOS CT
LAKE LURE CT
LAKE GEORGE
LAKE CLAIRE CT
SUCCESS PL

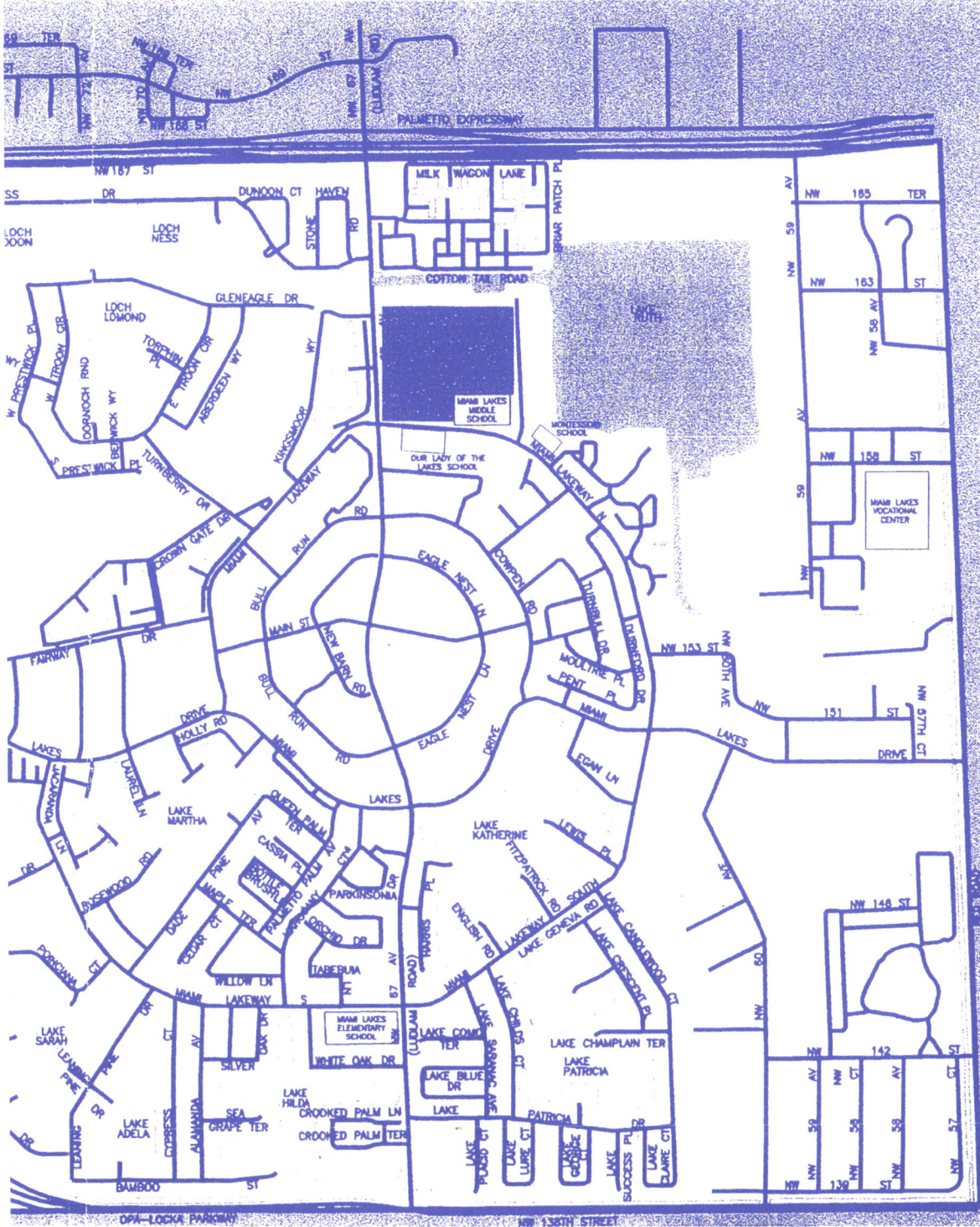

OPA-LOCKA PARKWAY
NW 138TH STREET

NW 57 AV
NW 58 AV
NW 59 AV

ISBN: 0-9820733-8-0
Miami Lakes From A to Z
Digitally reproduced in 2009 by
CONVERPAGE
23 Acorn Street
Scituate, MA 02066
781-378-1996

Miami Lakes

Dedicated to my daughter Andrea for her patience and enthusiasm as she helped prepare this book for publication.
Everyone needs an Andie!!

from A . . .

With special thanks to the town officials who generously shared their time and information with me. Also sincere gratitude to Roger Reese, Editor and James Lezcano of the Miami Laker, and to Stu Wyllie, President of The Graham Companies for reading and commenting on the content of this book. Last but not least, thanks to Sylvia of Impressions Hair Salon for sharing her memories of Miami Lakes.

. . . to Z!

TOWN OF MIAMI LAKES

INCORPORATED
DECEMBER 5, 2000

FLORIDA

The town seal was designed by Felicia Salazar. It incorporates the town's origin as a dairy farm, its tropical climate, the homes and open spaces of the present, as well as its flora and fauna.

A   a

alphabet   **architecture**   **art**

In Miami Lakes the letters of the **alphabet** can be found in both **architecture** and nature. Can you find the letter A in the roots of the tree in this picture? As you read <u>Miami Lakes from A to Z</u> try to find the designated letter in the picture on each page.

Many kinds of **artists** live in Miami Lakes. Some **artists** are actors, some are painters, some are sculptors and some are **architects**. There are also authors and singers. Can you name any **artists**?

There is **art** in every corner of Miami Lakes. The painted cows remind us that Miami Lakes was once a dairy farm. Murals decorate the walls of Miami Lakes Middle School and the history of the town is told in the wall mural in front of Gerardo's Marketplace off Main Street. The sculptures of the newsboy and sports figures at Don Shula's Hotel are imaginative and **artistic**. Even the mailboxes in town are **art**.

Q. What 8 letter word begins with A and ends with Z?
A. alphabet

B b

business   ball field   beach

Over 1700 **businesses** operate in the Miami Lakes community. Among those are stores, banks, barber shops, medical offices and light industry. Have you gone to any **businesses** in town today?

 The **ball fields** in town are used by both children and adults. The sports that are played on them include baseball, football and soccer. Some people like to play Frisbee on the fields.

Six **beach**-front parks are maintained by the Miami Lakes Park and Recreation Department. These swimming **beaches** are located on Lake Cynthia, Lake Glen Ellen, Lake Suzie, Lake Patricia, and two on Lake Hilda.

Q. What is the best way to raise blueberries?
A. With a spoon.

C c

cows   **celebrities**   **council**

The Town of Miami Lakes was developed on land that was formerly a dairy farm owned by Ernest "Cap" Graham. **Cows** roamed the land on which homes, schools, stores and churches sit today. Dairy **cows** continue to be pastured throughout the town, giving the area a rural look and feeling. When mature these Holstein **cows** are milked at the Graham Farms in Moore Haven, Florida.

The Town of Miami Lakes was incorporated on December 5, 2000. That means that it has a mayor-**council**-manager form of government. The **council** is made up of the mayor and six members. Together they have the legislative power in the town. The manager is responsible for overseeing all town affairs and enacting the policies of the **council**.

Did you know that some **celebrities** come from Miami Lakes? They are Senator Bob Graham, rapper Vanilla Ice, K.C. of K.C. and the Sunshine Band and Portland Trail Blazer basketball player, Steve Blake.

Q. Have you ever seen
1. a cat fish?
2. a horse fly?

D d

Dade **ducks** **diversity**

Miami Lakes is a municipality in Miami-**Dade** County. Although it has its own government, Miami Lakes is still reliant on the County for police, fire, waste-management and library services.

The **duck** most people notice in Miami Lakes is the Muscovy. Some think Muscovys are ugly because of the red warty area above the beak and around the eves. Muscovys can be beneficial. They eat mosquitoes and bugs. Muscovy **ducks** are fun to watch. Did you ever see a Muscovy wag its tail like a puppy dog?

There is a **diversity** of background, culture and language among the population in Miami Lakes. Residents come from Asia, Columbia, Cuba, Europe, Nicaragua, Venezuala and the Middle East. As of the year 2000, speakers of Spanish as a first language accounted for 72.4% of the population while English made up 24.7%.

Q. Name a key that is hard to turn.
A. a donkey

E e

education   entertainment   eagle

There seems to be something to enhance the lives of everyone in Miami Lakes. **Entertainment** includes Family Night Out on Main Street, movies, festivals, sports, the Main Street Players theater group and school activities.

Public school **education** in Miami Lakes is under the direction of Miami-Dade County. Miami Dade is the fourth largest school district in the United States. Soon Miami Dade College will establish the Miami Lakes Higher **Education** Academic Institute in town. A variety of credit and non-credit courses leading to an AS, AA or Vocational Certificate will be offered.

Eagles, our nation's symbol of freedom, once lived in Miami Lakes. **Eagle's** Nest Lane derives its name from the **eagles** that roosted on top of poles near Main Street. A nest of **eagles**, once an endangered species was recently spotted in the nearby town of Pembroke Pines. Will **eagles** return to Miami Lakes?

Fill in the blank with an anagram (same letters but different order) for the underlined word. If you want to reach <u>below</u> the table you must bend your _____.

A. elbow

5

F f

fountains   **flag**   **friendly**

Fountains are a signature of Miami Lakes. They are found both on public lands and private property. Visitors are welcomed into Miami Lakes with three **fountains:** an oak tree, a golfer, and a windmill. Can you find each of these fountains in town? The lovely blue tiled, ever-flowing **fountain** located on Main Street is a favorite gathering place in the center of town. People young and old come to the **fountain** to sit and chat.

The town **flag** flies in front of the Town Hall and the Miami Lakes Community Center. The **flag** has the town seal on a blue background.

Miami Lakes' mission statement declares that the town strives to be a "**friendly**, peaceful, safe and beautiful town whose residents and business leaders take pride in where they live, work and play."

Change the last letter in the word REFINE to D (REFIN_). Unscramble the letters to discover a pal.

A. friend

G g

Graham   geography   garden

The three **Graham** brothers, Philip, William and Robert, along with landscape architect and planner Lester Collins, developed the master plan for what would become the town of Miami Lakes. The **Grahams** were the sons of "Cap" **Graham**, a former state senator and owner of the **Graham** Dairy Farm. Philip was the publisher of The Washington Post and Newsweek, Bill was chairman of the **Graham** Companies and a breeder of Angus cattle, and Bob is a former Florida governor and U.S. Senator. In 2003, Senator **Graham** received an artificial replacement heart valve made from a Holstein cow's heart tissue.

Study of the **geography** of Miami Lakes shows that it is located between the Atlantic Ocean and the Everglades. It has a total area of 6.4 miles, .4 miles of which is water, and an elevation of 3 feet above sea level. Its climate is tropical. South Florida is the most likely area in the world to be struck by a hurricane.

Miami Lakes' median strips and islands are beautifully maintained **gardens.** Along with the tree canopy, these flowers add to the year-round beauty of the town. Butterfly **gardens** can be found at Miami Lakes Middle School, Our Lady of the Lakes Catholic School, Royal Oaks Park and on Miami Lakeway South.

Q. Why do monkeys bow to a giraffe?

A. Because he is called "your highness".

H h

house   **hometown**   **hurricane**

The history of Miami Lakes actually began in the 1930's when "Cap" Graham purchased his 3,000 acre dairy farm. This "ugly piece of land in Dade County" eventually became the vibrant and beautiful city of Miami Lakes, with 23 lakes, 99 parks, tree lined streets and a **hometown** atmosphere. During his Grand Opening Day speech on July 22, 1962 Philip Graham said, "We want people to say with pride that they live in Miami Lakes." Today we hear more and more people proudly say, "I grew up in Miami Lakes, it's my **hometown.**"

The first **houses** offered in Miami Lakes started at $13,850. These were two bedroom, one bath homes, with a garage and tile roof. The most expensive **house**, the Lake Placid, included a swimming pool and cost $23,900. Forty-five years later Miami Lakes' original homes could sell for as much as 20 times more.

Most **hurricanes** in South Florida occur between mid-August and the end of October. The major **hurricanes** to affect Miami Lakes since its founding were Andrew in 1992, Irene in 1999, and **Hurricanes** Katrina and Wilma in 2005. During Katrina 10 to 14 inches of rain fell in southern Florida. It was the most devastating hurricane in U.S. history. These **hurricanes** caused vast wind and water damage. Miami Lakes' homeowners lost roofs and the town's tree canopy was devastated. Years later the town is still working to restore the trees.

Q. If horses tell pony tales, what kind of stories do cows tell?   A. dairy tales.

I i

incorporation   iguana   imagine

Talks of **incorporation** began in 1995 by the Miami Lakes Civic Association. The idea was to secure the benefits of home rule, including the opportunity for public participation in local government. The Miami-Dade County Commission was concerned that **incorporation** of the Town of Miami Lakes would have a negative impact on tax payers in the remaining unincorporated areas. On September 19, 2000 the Board voted to authorize the creation of the Town of Miami Lakes, to include Royal Oaks and West Lake within its boundaries and to charge a mitigation fee. Wayne Slaton, the champion of the **incorporation** effort, was elected Miami Lakes' first Mayor.

Imagine Miami Lakes before it had its own government.
Imagine the Old Barn used as a recreation center and theater.
Imagine Santa Claus arriving on a fire truck for the tree lighting ceremony.
Imagine Main Street entertainers dressed up as Dickens Carolers.
Imagine cows pastured over 75% of the town.
Imagine deer, alligators, **iguanas**, and possums roaming throughout the area.
Imagine getting ice cream at Drexel's Dairy and seeing buffalo pastured nearby.
Imagine hard work and careful planning resulting in this beautiful community.

Q. What magazine do Dalmations read?   A. Spots Illustrated

J j

jingle   jacaranda   jungle gym

Jingle Down Main Street 5K Run and Walk is a holiday tradition in Miami Lakes. Each participant wears a timing chip and **jingle** bells in his/her shoes. Prizes, food and drinks await the runners and walkers at the end of the race.

Jacaranda and Tabebuia trees grow in Miami Lakes. The **Jacaranda** is recognized by its showy blue or violet flowers and oppositely paired, compound leaves. The Yellow Tabebuia tree is also called the Trumpet tree. It blooms early in the spring.   Tabebuia trees hold their leaves all winter then drop them just before blooming. Tabebuia grow well in South Florida because once established they are quite hardy and don't need a lot of water. To collect Tabebuia seeds, allow the seed heads to dry on the plant, then remove the seeds and sow as soon as possible, because they do not store well.

The numerous parks and tot-lots situated within walking distance of every neighborhood have different types of play equipment. **Jungle gyms** are a favorite for children who enjoy climbing, swinging, and sliding. The **jungle gyms** provide a wonderful outlet for youthful energy while building flexibility, balance, coordination, strength and imagination.

Q. On what side are a jaguar's spots?
A. the outside.

K k

kids   **key**   **Katharine**

The health, happiness and safety of **kids** have long been a priority in Miami Lakes. Tot-lots and pocket-parks were included in the original development plans. The Park and Recreation Department offers over 50 events per year, many of which are enrichment opportunities for **kids.** Movies in the Park, Concerts on the Fairway, The Bike Rodeo and Safety Day and The Safe Routes to School Program are but a few of the **kid** centered programs. The town and the Optimist Club are building the Boundless Playground for **kids** with special needs.

Did you know that there is a "**Key**" to the Town of Miami Lakes? The ornamental **key** is an honor bestowed on esteemed friends and members of the community. In medieval times the gates to walled cities were locked at night, so the **key** symbolizes the recipient's freedom to enter and leave the city at will. The "**Key** to the Town of Miami Lakes Scholarship Program" gives an official **Key** to two graduating seniors who have demonstrated academic excellence, leadership skills and extraordinary commitment to their school and community.

Lake **Katharine** is named for the wife of Philip Graham. Upon his death **Katharine** Graham became publisher of the Washington Post and later won the Pulitzer Prize for her memoirs.

Q. What has 88 keys that won't open anything?   A. piano

L l

lake   library   landscape

Lakes Patricia, Katharine, Hilda, Adele, Elizabeth, Carol, Cynthia, and Sandra were named after women in the Graham family. Lakes Sarah, Suzie, Martha and Glen Ellen were named for the Graham family friends. Lake Ruth was named for the wife of Andy Cappeletti, of the Cappeletti Company. The **lochs** in Miami **Lakes** honor the Graham's Scottish heritage.

Miami **Lakes** Branch **Library** is part of the Miami-Dade Public **Library** System. It opened in 1981 on land donated by The Graham Companies. Miami **Lakes** Branch **Library** serves a multilingual, multi-age community with books in several languages, internet access, audio and video materials, newspapers and magazines. Storytelling, musical presentations, arts and crafts are available for children. Adults and teens participate in clubs, discussion groups and tutoring.

Miami **Lakes'** homeowner's associations have **landscaping** requirements meant to keep neighborhoods neat and uniform. Town parks and public lands are kept beautifully **landscaped** with well-trimmed lawns and gardens. Miami **Lakes** residents are proud of the image they project as a small town with many **lakes**, a championship golf course and **landscaped** yards and public ways.

Q. A group of lions is called a pride, have you heard what a group of cows is called?   A. a herd

M m

Miami Lakes   **Main Street**   **map**

Development of the town of **Miami Lakes** was begun in 1962 by Sengra (now The Graham Companies) on land east of the Palmetto Expressway. The master plan for the area included curved tree-lined roadways and neighborhoods with their own shopping centers, parks and services. The plan included a championship golf course, an industrial district, schools, churches and zones for apartments and town houses. **Miami Lakes** was designed to be an all-encompassing community where both families and corporations could feel at home.

The town center is called **Main Street.** Designed as both a commercial and residential area, it has become a magnet for **Miami Lakes'** residents. **Main Street** is a social hub where people go to meet, shop, and eat as well as to enjoy art, music, craft shows, and all types of festivals.

The **map** of **Miami Lakes** has changed since the town was originally planned. In the time of incorporation the communities of Royal Oaks and West Lake were added to the town. Miami Lakes now covers 6.4 miles.

Fill in the blank with an anagram (same letters but different order) for the underlined word.

A lemon tastes sour, but a _____ tastes sweet.   A. melon

N n

neighborhood   new   northwest

In 1962 the **new** town of Miami Lakes opened its first model home. Miami Lakes, Florida is located in **northwest** Dade in the bend of the Palmetto Expressway. Dairy cows had to be moved and fenced in so houses could be built around the **new** Lake Patricia. Local cowboys proclaimed that the area was, "the end of nowhere." Now, more than forty-five years later, we know that they had misjudged both the accessibility and success of the **new** development.

This pedestrian-friendly, mixed-use town was built with 23 lakes nestled within the **neighborhoods**. Open spaces, landscaped streets, and tot-lots provide opportunities to enjoy the great outdoors. Nearby schools, churches and stores keep the **neighborhoods** cohesive, safe and friendly places to live.

Fill in the blank with an anagram (same letters but different order) for the underlined word.

When the scouts had <u>sewn</u> 100 blankets for the hurricane victims, their good deed was in the _____.

A. news

14

O   o

organizations   **oranges**   **optimists**

There are numerous clubs and **organizations** in Miami Lakes. Some are school and church related and some are more community oriented. These **organizations** offer opportunities for volunteers to lend their time and talent to the people of Miami Lakes. One such organization is the **Optimist** Club. The **Optimists** are serious about "Bringing Out the Best in Kids." The Club runs several sports programs for boys and girls, as well as sponsoring scholarships and contests. Like the Scouts, Rotary, Kiwanis and Lions Clubs the **Optimists** promote an active interest in good government and civic affairs and encourage participation in service to the community.

Because of its tropical climate, citrus fruits can grow well in Miami Lakes. Until 1995 when Citrus Canker disease was discovered in Florida, **orange**, grapefruit, and lime trees were frequently seen in people's yards. Citrus Canker disease causes premature leaf and fruit drop and makes the fruit too unsightly to eat or sell. Did you know that an **orange** seed is called a pip?

Q. When is it dangerous to go outdoors?   A. When it is raining cats and dogs.

P p

parks   **plan**   **play**

The master **plan** for Miami Lakes included many **parks** and green areas. The **planners** recognized the importance of **play** and leisure in a totally integrated community. Large **parks** provided areas to **play** group sports, while young children could **play** close to home.

The **Parks** and Recreation Department maintains clean, safe and attractive grounds, structures and facilities. The **Park** Department strives to provide activities and recreation for the enjoyment of all Miami Lakes residents.

There are 99 **park** locations within the 6.4 mile radius of Miami Lakes. Since 1965 the **Parks** Department's area of responsibility has grown from five acres to over 260 acres. Within this area are the six beach front **parks,** 93 tot-lot **parks**, 2 picnic **parks**, 68 miles of greenery, cul-de-sacs, median strips, and more than 15,000 trees. Animals and motorized vehicles are not allowed in the **parks**.

Light industry and office **parks** are an integral part of the town. The business **parks** are located on the east and west boundaries of the town. They provide employment for many Miami Lakes' residents.

Say this 3 times fast: Pink panthers proudly planting prickly purple pumpkins!

Q q

quiet   **quality**   **quilt**

Miami Lakes is a **quiet** town. Its tree-lined streets, local parks and curving roads keep the neighborhoods safe and nearly traffic free. The small town atmosphere within commuting distance of the city of Miami, make it a **quiet** oasis in which to live and bring up a family. **Quiet** and quaintness contribute to the high **quality** of life for Miami Lakes' residents and visitors.

Seamstresses and **quilters** live in the Miami Lakes area. **Quilting** is a very old art form used to provide blankets for warmth and decoration. Young girls made **quilts** for their trousseau and kept them in a hope chest until they were married. A **quilt** was an inexpensive way to use up scraps and surplus fabric. **Quilts** were often used in the maker's home or sold to bring in extra income.

 Recently several **quilters** formed a group called "**Quilts** for Kids." They sew **quilts** to give comfort to children in local hospitals. What a wonderful way for area **quilters** to share their love for **quilting.**

Riddle: Have you ever seen?

      1. a quarter horse   2. a kitty litter

17

R r

red   **rain**   **recreation**

When you visit Miami Lakes you may see "**red**"!
Red Road, the eastern boundary of Miami Lakes.
Red brick sidewalks on Main Street.
Red tile roofs.
Red in local landscaping, (croton, hibiscus, begonia, and bottlebrush).
Red stripe on the American flag and **Red** cross on the Florida state flag.
What are some things around Miami Lakes that make you see "**red**"?

The average **rainfall** in Miami Lakes is 66.04 inches per year, while in the U.S. the average is 37 inches. Miami Lakes has 132 days of meaningful precipitation. June is the wettest month. Using a **rain** barrel is an inexpensive way to capture and store water that can be used later for irrigating the landscape.

Opportunities for outdoor **recreation** abound in Miami Lakes. The town boasts two large and attractive picnic parks, six town beaches, and the new town marina at Miami Lakes Optimist Park. Organized sports are run by the schools, the Optimist Club and the **Recreation** Department. The skate park on Miami Lakes Drive East, with ramps, grind rails and obstacles is a safe place for local skateboarders and rollerbladers to practice. The golf course and tennis and basketball courts are available. All the residents of Miami Lakes can find a special way to rest or exercise in order to enjoy life in this extraordinary town.

Can you change the word READ to BEND by changing one letter at a time?

A. READ
REED
SEED
SEND
BEND

18

S s

street　　　　　　**seal**　　　　　　**Sengra**

The **Sengra** Development Corporation did not lay out the **streets** in Miami Lakes in grids as they are in the Miami area. The **streets** are curvilinear, designed to slow traffic and offer residents safe and quiet neighborhoods.

Miami Lakes' **streets** have interesting names. The "Tree **Streets**" are located south of Miami Lakes Drive. Jacaranda Lane, Holly Road, Rosewood Drive, Palmetto Palm Avenue, and Mahogany and Cedar Courts encircle Lake Martha. The **streets** around Lake Katharine (Egan Lane, Lewis, Fitzpatrick and English Roads) were named to honor the first Miami landowners. Many of Miami Lakes' **streets** have dairy farm related names (New Barn Road, Bull Run and Cow Pen Road). Can you find other patterns in the naming of **streets** in Miami Lakes?

The **town seal** shows the sun shining on a sailboat on a blue lake surrounded by green grass, houses, palm trees, cows and a great blue heron. There is a banner that proclaims Town of Miami Lakes Incorporated December 3, 2000. The **seal** is displayed on official structures, vehicles, signs and correspondence. Have you ever walked on the town **seal**? You can if you go to the Town Hall where offices have the town **seal** on the doormats.

Say this fast: Silly Sally sips salty soda slowly.

T t

town   **tree**   **technology**

Miami Lakes is a **town** with a difference. It was designed to be built over an extended period which would allow for changing times and conditions. It was to be a self-contained community with a diverse range of housing, job opportunities and amenities, all within walking distance of the residences. The architecture and landscaping would take advantage of the local climate and ecology. When explaining the need for a new **town** in south Florida, Bill Graham said, "Growth has made it necessary to provide more for people than for cows."

Miami Lakes has moved into the age of **technology**. There are computers in schools and in the library. Wi-Fi spots are available throughout town, including the parks, the library, hotels, and restaurants.

 "**Tree** City USA" is a designation granted to Miami Lakes by the National Arbor Day Foundation on November 28, 2007. To celebrate this honor the town planted its 550th live oak **tree** within the town limits. The town is busily restoring the **tree** canopy ravished by Hurricane Wilma in 2005.

Can you change the word TREE to SLED by changing one letter at a time?

A. TREE
   FREE
   FLEE
   FLED
   SLED

20

U u

urbanism   **unique**   **unite**

Miami Lakes is an example of **unique** and innovative town planning. It is a model of the "New **Urbanism**," that is a planned self-contained community, diverse in use and population. The word **urban** usually conjures up visions of a busy and congested city, but the "New **Urbanism**" concept is one of quiet neighborhoods and local parks with easy accessibility to shopping and conveniences.

Think of Miami Lakes with its striped awnings and tiled roofs, tree canopy and open spaces, this is truly a **unique** oasis within the heart of bustling South Florida.

The architecture, landscaping, parks and central Miami Dade location **unite** to make Miami Lakes a wonderful hometown, a place where residents take pride in where they live, work and play. Miami Lakes is a **united** community, with opportunities to gather, worship, learn and celebrate. No wonder it is home to over 27,000 residents

Fill in the blank with an anagram (different word but same letters) for the underlined word.
Q. The cows will all <u>unite</u> if the farmer will _____ the rope on the gate.   A. untie

V v

vision   veteran   volunteer

The developers of Miami Lakes had a **vision** of a community of beautiful homes, curving streets, man-made lakes and tree-lined roadways. That **vision** has now become a well-established town with its own government, schools, churches, and places to work and play.

Veterans are those who served in our country's armed forces. They are formally honored on November 11th, but should be remembered and respected throughout the year. The annual **Veteran's** Day Parade honors our **veterans** with marching bands, clowns, floats, scouts, dignitaries and, of course, lots of American flags.

Miami Lakes offers many opportunities for **volunteers** to serve the community. School and church groups, and local organizations **volunteer** to provide help for those less fortunate and to run sports and community events. The Halloween Haunted House, the Festival of Lights, and weekly entertainment on Main Street are just a few examples of the safe and fun activities **volunteers** make possible. Boy Scouts **volunteer** to run Santa's Workshop, giving children a chance to buy gifts for their families and raises money for the Scouts Summer Camp Fund.

Fill in the blank with an anagram (same letters but different order) for the underlined word.
Put water in the vase if you want to _____ the flowers.   A: save

W w

water   work   welcoming

The **water** in Miami Lakes is obtained directly from the Miami-Dade **Water** and Sewer Department. This **water** supply comes from the Biscayne Aquifer which is located just below the surface of the land in South Florida. The land is made of porous rock. **Water** is filtered as it seeps in and fills the tiny cracks and holes. The **water** is generally clean due to the effects of this natural filtration.

The town plan included commercial areas so residents could **work** near where they live. To date 13% of the town's area is used for light industry and office parks. Over 14,000 people are employed by more than 250 companies located in Miami Lakes. There are more than 17,000 businesses in the town. The Graham Companies is still the largest property owners in Miami Lakes, owning Shula's Athletic Club, Don Shula's Golf Club, 1,500 rental apartments, and more than two million square feet of office, industrial and retail space.

Miami Lakes is a warm and **welcoming** town. Visitors experience the fun and excitement of small town charm, big town amenities and a plethora of activities and entertainment. Remember that the Miami Lakes mission is to be a "friendly, peaceful, safe and beautiful town whose residents and business leaders take pride in where they live, **work** and play."

Q. What gets wetter and wetter as it dries?   A. a towel

X x

x   X ing   example

X is a very versatile letter because it can mean many things. For **eXample**, **X** can mark the spot on a treasure map. It can be used in place of a signature or to indicate a choice on a test or a survey.

In math, **X** is often used to indicate an unknown factor or number. A small **x** in a math equation means multiply. **X** is the Roman numeral for the number 10, so Super Bowl 43 is written "Super Bowl **X**LIII."

X is a short way to write "cross." Sometimes a yellow circle with an **X** in the middle and an "R" on each side tells drivers, "Danger, Railroad Crossing," be prepared to stop, look and listen.

Another way to say crossing is **Xing**. **X** on a street sign means caution, pedestrians, animals or a train is crossing. Did you ever see a sign that said "Holstein **Xing**" or "Alligators **Xing**"?

Can you change the word BAT to FOX by changing one letter at a time?

BAT
BA<u>Y</u>
B<u>O</u>Y
BO<u>X</u>
<u>F</u>OX

24

Y y

youth   **yesterday**   **years**

Yesterday pastureland for grazing cattle; today an area of lakes and parks.
Yesterday cow paths; today paved streets and sidewalks.
Yesterday barns; today homes, schools, churches and businesses.
Yesterday water and food troughs; today restaurants and grocery stores.
Yesterday a dream of a community of homes, lakes and tree lined streets.
Today a reality.

Many letters in this book tell about Miami Lakes' past, but that was **yesterday** and **yesterday's** gone. 1962 seems like only **yesterday** to those who have lived in town for many **years**, but in 2012 Miami Lakes will celebrate its 50 **year** anniversary. Today's **youth** will learn from the past and help Miami Lakes continue to grow and change into the town of tomorrow.

What do you think Miami Lakes will look like in 50 **years**?

Q. When is a yacht not a yacht?   A. When it's asea.

25

Z z

zone   **zip code**   **zero**

Zip Code or **Zone** Improvement Plan is a 5 digit system used by the U.S. Post Office to facilitate the sorting and delivery of mail. The first digit represents one of ten regions of the country. The number three is for the southeast. The next two numbers indicate a regional center or main post office, and the last two digits represent small post offices or postal **zones** in larger **zoned** cities. Miami Lake's Zip Code is 33 **zero**14.

Zip north and south, zip east and west. What letters did you find in Miami Lakes today?

Q. What is black and white and red all over?

A. an embarrassed zebra

26

A a

H h

B b

I i

C c

J j

D d

K k

E e

L l

F f

M m

G g

N n

O o

U u

P p

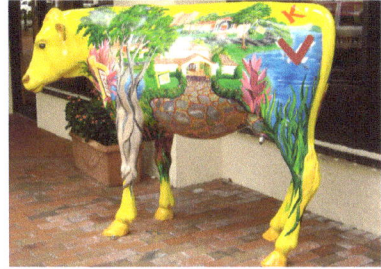

V v

Q q

W w

R r

X x

S s

Y y

T t

Z z

Gael (Sullivan) Daly has been coming to Miami Lakes for over thirty years. She now enjoys Miami Lakes as a year round resident with her husband Timothy. Their 8 children and 14 grandchildren all love to visit and enjoy Miami Lakes' fun and beauty.

As an Elementary School Reading Specialist for over 35 years, Gael shared her love of Children's Literature and reading with hundreds of students and numerous colleagues. Concept Books have long been a favorite genre as she has marveled at the many different shapes and forms ABC books can take.

For Gael, it was a joy writing and photographing ***Miami Lakes From A to Z***. "Wandering through the alphabet with my readers is both a privilege and a pleasure!" She is also the author of ***Scituate From A to Z.***

abcbook@comcast.net

www.ingramcontent.com/pod-product-compliance
Lightning Source LLC
Chambersburg PA
CBHW041548040426
42447CB00002B/97